The Unseen Realm

An Introduction to The Realm Of The Supernatural

(UNSEEN REALM BOOK 1)

FRANCIS JONAH

Contents

INTRODUCTION

CHAPTER ONE:

CHAPTER TWO:

CHAPTER THREE:

CHAPTER FOUR:

CHAPTER FIVE:

IMPORTANT

My name is Francis Jonah. I believe all things are possible. It is because of this belief that I have achieved so much in life. This belief extends to all. I believe every human being is equipped to succeed in every circumstance, regardless of the circumstance.

I know the only gap that exists between you and what you need to achieve or overcome is knowledge.

People are destroyed for lack of knowledge.

It is for this reason that I write short practical books that are so simple, people begin to experience immediate results as evidenced by the many testimonies I receive on daily basis for my various books.

This book is no exception. You will obtain results because of it.

FREE GIFT

Just to say Thank You for downloading my book, I'd like to give you these books for free.

Download these 4 powerful books today for free and give yourself a great future

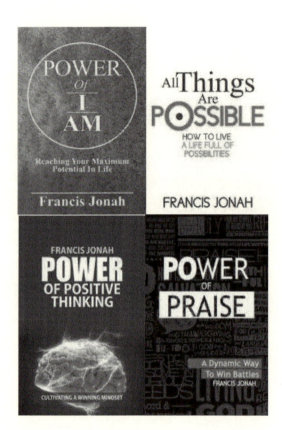

Click Here To Download

Counselling Or Prayer

Send me an email if you need prayer or counsel or you have a question.

Better still if you want to make my acquaintance

My email is drfrancisjonah@gmail.com

INTRODUCTION

The unseen realm can simply be defined as the realm of life beyond what we can see with our eyes.

Though we do not see it, we are made to know in the word of God that it exists.

We are also made to know that it is the realm from which the physical realm we live in emanated.

The scriptures put it like this:

Through faith we understand that the worlds were framed by the word of God, so that things

which are seen were not made of things which do appear.

Hebrews 11:3

The worlds were made of things which are not seen. They were not made of things that do appear. They were made of things that are not seen, that do not appear.

This is too powerful.

For the worlds to be created by the unseen or supernatural, it tells us that there is so much power in that realm.

The Bible makes us understand that the things in the realm of the unseen are also eternal.

Eternal means they are permanent. Glory. I am confident we want to see some permanent things in our lives. See what the Bible says:

While we look not at the things which are seen, but at the things which are not seen: for the things which are seen are temporal; but the things which are not seen are eternal. 2Corinthians 4:18

The scripture clearly says that we are to look at the unseen and give little attention to the seen.

The sad reality is that a lot of us are looking at the seen realm and have not even perceived the unseen realm.

Today, it will change to the glory of God.

We know that there is the seen realm and the unseen realm.

This book is a short book and an introduction to the realm of the unseen. Although it contains powerful revelations and testimonies, it must be read in the context of it being an introduction to the unseen realm.

Let us delve deeper into our introduction of the unseen realm.

CHAPTER ONE:

ELEMENTS IN THE UNSEEN

When we talk of the unseen, a lot of people limit themselves to angels.

They want to see angels and then they will be satisfied.

The truth of the matter though is that the unseen realm has so many other elements that can transform the life of the believer.

We must identify these elements and magnify their effects in our lives.

With a great understanding of these elements, all believers will walk in higher levels of His glory.

The unseen

Our world is not only physical, there is a spiritual dimension to it.

It is the realm where God, the angels, demons and other beings operate.

It is the most powerful realm that exists and mastery of that realm will automatically make any one a master in the realm of the physical.

We are already aware that the physical world came from the spiritual world.

Here is an account where you see the spiritual bring the natural into being:

Gen 1:26 And God said, Let us make man in our image, after our likeness: and let them have dominion over the fish of the sea, and over the fowl of the air, and over the cattle, and over all the earth, and over every creeping thing that creepeth upon the earth.

Gen 1:27 So God created man in his own image, in the image of God created he him; male and female created he them.

Gen 1:28 And God blessed them, and God said unto them, Be fruitful, and multiply, and replenish the earth, and subdue it: and have dominion over the fish of the sea, and over the fowl of the air, and over every living thing that moveth upon the earth.

Genesis 1:26-28

This scripture clearly shows you that there are different realms of life.

One day, Daniel had an experience where he was battling on earth in fasting and prayer, and that same battle was happening in the spirit realm.

The account is worthy of note:

Dan 10:1 In the third year of Cyrus king of Persia a thing was revealed unto Daniel, whose name was called Belteshazzar; and the thing was true, but the time appointed was long: and he understood the thing, and had understanding of the vision.

Dan 10:2 In those days I Daniel was mourning three full weeks.

Dan 10:3 I ate no pleasant bread, neither came flesh nor wine in my mouth, neither did I anoint myself at all, till three whole weeks were fulfilled.

Dan 10:4 And in the four and twentieth day of the first month, as I was by the side of the great river, which is Hiddekel;

Dan 10:5 Then I lifted up mine eyes, and looked, and behold a certain man clothed in linen, whose loins were girded with fine gold of Uphaz:

Dan 10:6 His body also was like the beryl, and his face as the appearance of lightning, and his eyes as lamps of fire, and his arms and his feet like in colour to polished brass, and the voice of his words like the voice of a multitude.

Dan 10:7 And I Daniel alone saw the vision: for the men that were with me saw not the vision; but a great quaking fell upon them, so that they fled to hide themselves.

Dan 10:8 Therefore I was left alone, and saw this great vision, and there remained no strength in me: for my comeliness was turned in me into corruption, and I retained no strength.

Dan 10:9 Yet heard I the voice of his words: and when I heard the voice of his words, then was I in a deep sleep on my face, and my face toward the ground.

Dan 10:10 And, behold, an hand touched me, which set me upon my knees and upon the palms of my hands.

Dan 10:11 And he said unto me, O Daniel, a man greatly beloved, understand the words that I speak unto thee, and stand upright: for unto thee am I now sent. And when he had spoken this word unto me, I stood trembling.

Dan 10:12 Then said he unto me, Fear not, Daniel: for from the first day that thou didst set thine heart to understand, and to chasten thyself before thy God, thy words were heard, and I am come for thy words.

Dan 10:13 But the prince of the kingdom of Persia withstood me one and twenty days: but, lo, Michael, one of the chief princes, came to help me; and I remained there with the kings of Persia.

Dan 10:14 Now I am come to make thee understand what shall befall thy people in the latter days: for yet the vision is for many days.

Daniel 10:1-14

Whiles Daniel prayed and fasted, there was another battle in the unseen realm.

Finally, the angel Gabriel came from the realm of the spirit to deliver a message to Daniel in the realm of the physical.

This brief introduction of the seen and unseen realms is a good foundation to build upon.

Now that we know of the unseen realm, let us go deeper into the elements that operate in the unseen realm.

These are tools that will help anyone master that realm of life.

Below are some unseen elements. Although they are unseen, their impact is always seen in the physical, in the lives of human beings and other creatures of God.

1. Blessing

No one has seen the blessing of God, but this blessing does great things.

It elevated people like Abraham, Isaac and Jacob and made them so blessed in their generations that people envied them.

The scripture put it this way:

Then Isaac sowed in that land, and received in the same year an hundredfold: and the LORD blessed him.

And the man waxed great, and went forward, and grew until he became very great:

For he had possession of flocks, and possession of herds, and great store of servants: and the Philistines envied him.

Gen 26:12-14

This is too powerful, the Lord blessed Isaac with an unseen blessing and it made people envy him.

The unseen blessing is powerful indeed.

No wonder the Bible says:

The blessing of the LORD, it maketh rich, and he addeth no sorrow with it.

Proverbs 10:22

The blessing of God really makes rich. I have the blessing. You have the blessing too. Do not wait to see it with your eyes before you believe you have it. It is an unseen element, believe you have it.

And press on in prayer to manifest it more and more in your life.

The blessing of God will do you good in Jesus name.

2. Favour

Favour is an unseen element. Those who enjoyed it did great exploits in their generation.

For any man to be great in his generation, the element of favour is required.

Jesus required the element of favour to achieve his destiny. The scriptures say:

And Jesus increased in wisdom and stature, and in favour with God and man.

 Luke 2:52

Even Jesus our saviour increased in favour with both God and man.

He needed that unseen element of favour to fulfil his purpose. No one sees favour with their eyes, but we can all attest to it in the life of people.

This favour upon Jesus gave him helpers in ministry. It gave him someone to help him carry his cross.

It gave him someone to anoint his body for burial with an alabaster jar of perfume.

Favour gave him a free tomb to be buried in.

Mary could only qualify to be the mother of our saviour because she operated in high favour.

There is a certain level of favour required to operate at certain levels and positions in life.

Watch the verses as they unravel the mystery of the unseen element of high favour:

And the angel came in unto her, and said, Hail, thou that art highly favoured, the Lord is with thee: blessed art thou among women.

Luke 1:28

The angel said she was highly favoured. That high favour made her blessed among women. See the element of high favour working.

Favour will separate you from your equals in Jesus name.

There are different levels of favour.

It is your responsibility in prayer to demand to enjoy higher levels of favour.

There is favour and there is high favour.

Never be satisfied at your level of favour. Be diligent in prayer to walk in higher realms of favour.

Let us go on to learn about more unseen elements.

CHAPTER TWO:

MORE UNSEEN ELEMENTS

The unseen elements as stated are many.

Another element of the unseen realm is words.

3. Words

Words cannot be seen but their effects are unimaginable.

They have so much power that the Bible says they can kill or give life.

See:

Death and life *are* in the power of the tongue: and

they that love it shall eat the fruit thereof.

Proverbs 18:21

The tongue produces words and these carry life and death.

We have not yet realized the power of this great element of the unseen realm.

Words are so powerful that Jesus spoke them and dead people rose.

The account is here:

Then they took away the stone *from the place* **where the dead was laid. And Jesus lifted up** *his* **eyes, and said,** Father, I thank thee that thou hast heard me.

And I knew that thou hearest me always: but because of the people which stand by I said *it,* that they may believe that thou hast sent me.

And when he thus had spoken, he cried with a loud voice, Lazarus, come forth.

And he that was dead came forth, bound hand and foot with graveclothes: and his face was bound about with a napkin. Jesus saith unto them, Loose him, and let him go.

John 11:41-44

We must understand the power of the unseen element of words, for by it the worlds were created.

May your words always produce great and massive results in the realm of the physical. In Jesus name.

The words of Jesus stopped the wind

One day the wind was raging and tried to kill Jesus and his disciples.

Jesus was asleep by then.

He was awoken and he immediately rebuked the wind.

By some supernatural force, the winds were tamed by his words.

Your words will also tame circumstances against you in Jesus name.

Read the story here:

Mar 4:35 And the same day, when the even was come, he saith unto them, Let us pass over unto the other side.

Mar 4:36 And when they had sent away the multitude, they took him even as he was in the ship. And there were also with him other little ships.

Mar 4:37 And there arose a great storm of wind,

and the waves beat into the ship, so that it was now full.

Mar 4:38 And he was in the hinder part of the ship, asleep on a pillow: and they awake him, and say unto him, Master, carest thou not that we perish?

Mar 4:39 And he arose, and rebuked the wind, and said unto the sea, Peace, be still. And the wind ceased, and there was a great calm.

Mark 4:35-39

Words are powerful. They are unseen but produce massive results.

As you begin to use words, may they transform difficult situations in your life.

Read this testimony

I should have sent this in before now, but in December '09, a lightning strike began a bushfire on our property. The fire burned for close to a week. On the fourth day of the fire our home was threatened. At no time did we feel the need to evacuate. Instead, we had a reassurance within our spirits to stand and fight this natural force spiritually. My daughters and I stood on our house verandah rebuking the fire in Jesus' Name. We were reminded of when Jesus calmed the stormy waters, and knew we have that same power available to us because of His Name and His blood. Even the fire trucks raced to our home and waited for several hours as the fire sat on the mountaintop right before our home. Eventually they moved to another part of the property as the out-of-control fire just sat unmoving. It was as if an unseen wall was between our home and the fire. We give thanks to God for our home being saved and no injuries to the fire crews fighting the fires over that week.

4. Power

The power of God cannot be seen but its effects are still a mystery to many.

Jesus made us know we will have that power after the Holy Ghost is come upon us.

But ye shall receive power, after that the Holy Ghost is come upon you: and ye shall be witnesses unto me both in Jerusalem, and in all Judaea, and in Samaria, and unto the uttermost part of the earth.

Acts 1:8

The power is not seen with eyes. It is an unseen element but its reality is present with us.

The power of God is healing the sick, cleansing lepers, raising the dead, casting out demons.

The power is not seen with eyes but the results are tangible.

He gave the power in this manner:

And when he had called unto *him* his twelve disciples, he gave them power *against* unclean spirits, to cast them out, and to heal all manner of sickness and all manner of disease. Matthew 10:1

Nothing physical transpired. Only words were transferred.

Then the following instructions followed:

Heal the sick, cleanse the lepers, raise the dead, cast out devils: freely ye have received, freely give.

Matthew 10:8

The results of that supernatural element of power are littered through the Bible.

The disciples came one day to testify of that power:

Luk 10:17 And the seventy returned again with joy, saying, Lord, even the devils are subject unto us through thy name.

Luke 10:17

You will also walk in power in Jesus name. That power is in you.

God promised it to you. If you are not walking in it or you are walking in limited levels of power, go into prayer and fasting and press into more power. It is available unto you.

The Bible clearly says:

Luk 10:19 Behold, I give unto you power to tread on serpents and scorpions, and over all the power of the enemy: and nothing shall by any means hurt you.

Luke 10:19

CHAPTER THREE:

MORE UNSEEN ELEMENTS

I am sure you are now seeing a lot of the elements we have taken for granted.

Here are two more:

5. Righteousness

Righteousness is right standing before God.

It gives us the ability to stand before God without any sense of guilt and shame.

It gives us boldness to approach God.

By His special grace, this element of the unseen realm is a gift.

For if by one man's offence death reigned by one; much more they which receive abundance of grace and of the gift of righteousness shall reign in life by one, Jesus Christ.)

Romans 5:17

This powerful element that allows us to step into the presence of God at any time is a gift. Glory to God.

How do we receive that gift? Just believe and confess it. That is receiving by faith, another unseen element.

See how our righteousness is a gift and not of works. God is merciful.

But now the righteousness of God without the law is manifested, being witnessed by the law and the prophets;

Even the righteousness of God which is by faith of Jesus Christ unto all and upon all them that believe: for there is no difference:

Romans 3:21-22

How we have neglected this powerful element of the unseen realm.

6. Faith

By this element of the unseen, the elders obtained a good report.

The Bible makes us understand that by this element, those who have gone before us obtained good reports.

To obtain good reports too, we must give heed to and cultivate this powerful element of the unseen realm.

Now faith is the substance of things hoped for, the evidence of things not seen.
For by it the elders obtained a good report.
Hebrews 11:1-2

The bible says that is the only way believers must live, by this element of faith.

See:

For therein is the righteousness of God revealed

from faith to faith: as it is written, The just shall live by faith.

Romans 1:17

Without this same element, it is impossible to please God.

Hear it in the word of God:

***But without faith** it is **impossible to please** him: for he that cometh to God must believe that he is, and that he is a rewarder of them that diligently seek him.*

Hebrews 11:6

From today may faith be a powerful dimension in your life.

CHAPTER FOUR:

POTENCY OF THE UNSEEN REALM

The unseen realm is so powerful that whoever underestimates it does so at their own peril.

There is so much happening around us that we do not see. If we are to limit our lives therefore to what we see, we become very limited in life.

It is the reason the Bible says we the just must live by faith and not sight.

2Co 5:7 *(For we walk by faith, not by sight:)*

2 Corinthians 5:7

Is it not interesting that even the world we live in was created by the unseen and thus the unseen controls it?

These are clues of the potency of the unseen realm and the reason we must take advantage of that realm.

Heb 11:3 Through faith we understand that the worlds were framed by the word of God, so that things which are seen were not made of things which do appear.

Hebrews 11:3

The things which are seen came from things which are not seen.

The world we live in physically came from a realm that is not seen.

The influence of the unseen is so powerful that men who have understood it and are operating in that realm have become masters in their generation.

Masters over elements of the weather, diseases, death, financial circumstances, national and international problems.

JESUS DEALT WITH THE UNSEEN

Most of the diseases Jesus dealt with were caused directly by evil spirits and demons.

Although these are unseen, they have afflicted and tormented lots of people and killed many.

Sadly, many do not even have an idea of the seriousness of the damage this unseen evil forces cause in their lives.

Jn 3:8 He that committeth sin is of the devil; for the devil sinneth from the beginning. For this purpose the Son of God was manifested, that he might destroy the works of the devil.

1 John 3:8

Many have not seen the devil before. He is unseen to the physical eye. Yet, his impact in destruction and evil is unparalleled in this seen realm of ours.

By the grace of God, I have seen the devil as he confronted me one day in a vision. He was not able to do anything to me.

He was powerless in my presence. That experience helped build my confidence in the protection of God.

Even Jesus was manifested to destroy the works of the unseen in the realm of the seen. You neglect the realities of the unseen at your own peril.

The devil is working behind the scenes in a lot of situations and believers must stand to deal with him.

We have been given power over him and his works. We must not turn blind eyes to this reality.

Luk 10:19 Behold, I give unto you power to tread on serpents and scorpions, and over all the power of the enemy: and nothing shall by any means hurt you.

Luke 10:19

Jesus Himself said we had power over the devil and his works.

DEMONS CAUSED SICKNESS

Many of the diseases we see today are influenced and caused by spirits.

In the life of Jesus, he dealt with a lot of them. When he cast the unseen spirit out, the sicknesses and diseases also left.

It tells you that these spirits were the source of the diseases.

Mat 17:18 And Jesus rebuked the devil; and he departed out of him: and the child was cured from that very hour.

Matthew 17:18

After Jesus rebuked the devil, the child was cured. The unseen devil had afflicted the child with a serious case of epilepsy.

Medicine would never have cured this child because the root of his disease was unseen.

Mar 9:25 When Jesus saw that the people came running together, he rebuked the foul spirit, saying unto him, Thou dumb and deaf spirit, I charge thee, come out of him, and enter no more into him.

Mar 9:26 And the spirit cried, and rent him sore, and came out of him: and he was as one dead; insomuch that many said, He is dead.

Mar 9:27 But Jesus took him by the hand, and lifted him up; and he arose.

Mark 9:25-27

This person who was brought was deaf and dumb. Many who are not trained in the unseen realm would think it normal.

Not Jesus, He knew there was an unseen spirit behind the affliction.

After casting away the foul spirit, the person who was deaf and dumb could now hear and speak.

Glory to God.

Do not be deceived by the enemy. The unseen realm is potent and powerful and many things are happening in that realm.

OUR BATTLE IS IN THE UNSEEN

Our battle here on earth has never been physical. It has always been unseen.

It is one of the reasons too many people are failing. They are fighting in the wrong realm of life.

They are fighting in the physical when the battle is spiritual. Note what the Bible says:

2Co 10:3 For though we walk in the flesh, we do not war after the flesh:

2Co 10:4 (For the weapons of our warfare are not carnal, but mighty through God to the pulling down of strong holds;)

2 Corinthians 10:3-4

We are not fighting flesh and blood, our battle and warfare is spiritual. It is unseen.

Our weapons are also not carnal or fleshly. They are spiritual. Many believers are fighting with carnal weapons and getting nothing done.

If we can only switch to the realm of the unseen, things will become so much easier for us.

Glory to God for today. We have realised the existence and importance of the unseen realm and we must be ready to engage that realm for continuous victory.

SIMPLE VICTORY BY APPLYING LAWS OF THE UNSEEN

When the king of Moab was losing the battle to the Israelites, he switched to the unseen realm. He offered his eldest son as a sacrifice to his gods.

This invoked the spiritual on his behalf and caused him to survive a battle he should have been defeated and killed in.

The unseen is too powerful to be ignored. Brothers and sisters, let us equip ourselves with the right knowledge to prevail in that realm.

2Ki 3:26 And when the king of Moab saw that the battle was too sore for him, he took with him seven hundred men that drew swords, to break through even unto the king of Edom: but they could not.

2Ki 3:27 Then he took his eldest son that should have reigned in his stead, and offered him for a burnt offering upon the wall. And there was great indignation against Israel: and they departed from him, and returned to their own land.

2 Kings 3:26-27

BY STRENGTH SHALL NO MAN PREVAIL

Human strength has its limits. The elements of the seen are limited. They have what they can do. There are many things that are impossible in the seen realm.

For a life of limitless possibilities, we must operate in the unseen realm as much as possible.

The supernatural is what it takes to have victories that confound and confuse enemies.

1Sa 2:9 He will keep the feet of his saints, and the wicked shall be silent in darkness; for by strength shall no man prevail.

1 Samuel 2:9

If you really want to prevail in life, stop relying on your human strength and switch to the supernatural, it is so much easier and more glorious.

CHAPTER FIVE:

INFLUENCING THE UNSEEN REALM

With the elements we have discovered, there must be a way to take advantage of them.

Any man or woman who can influence the unseen realm is in for great triumphs.

Joshua stopped the sun one day till he won a battle he was involved in.

Whatever unseen hand that held the sun, I cannot tell but I know he influenced the realm of the unseen using an element of the unseen realm.

See the account:

Then spake Joshua to the LORD in the day when the LORD delivered up the Amorites before the children of Israel, and he said in the sight of Israel, Sun, stand thou still upon Gibeon; and thou, Moon, in the valley of Ajalon.

And the sun stood still, and the moon stayed, until the people had avenged themselves upon their enemies. Is not this written in the book of Jasher? So the sun stood still in the midst of heaven, and hasted not to go down about a whole day.

And there was no day like that before it or after it, that the LORD hearkened unto the voice of a man: for the LORD fought for Israel.

Joshua 10:12-14

This is so powerful.

The sun stopped for him to fight. We can see some

elements of the unseen he used.

They include:

Faith

He believed when told the sun to stand it, would stand.

He knew it would stand and commanded the sun to stand in the presence of all Israel.

This is bold faith. And many people achieved great things through the unseen element of faith.

The Bible says:

Heb 11:31 By faith the harlot Rahab perished not with them that believed not, when she had received the spies with peace.

Heb 11:32 And what shall I more say? for the time would fail me to tell of Gedeon, and of Barak, and

of Samson, and of Jephthae; of David also, and Samuel, and of the prophets:

Heb 11:33 Who through faith subdued kingdoms, wrought righteousness, obtained promises, stopped the mouths of lions,

Heb 11:34 Quenched the violence of fire, escaped the edge of the sword, out of weakness were made strong, waxed valiant in fight, turned to flight the armies of the aliens.

Hebrews 11:31-34

Glory to God. Faith always works.

Joshua applied his faith and it brought him results.

The second element he used was words.

Words

Words are powerful as we have seen earlier.

The way we use them is also very important.

In this very case, Joshua used words to command the sun to stand, not to beg it.

It reminds me of Jesus asking as to speak to the mountain.

Command the mountain to go, do not beg God to take it away.

Glory. Joshua used words and accomplished much.

Mar 11:23 For verily I say unto you, That whosoever shall say unto this mountain, Be thou removed, and be thou cast into the sea; and shall not doubt in his heart, but shall believe that those things which he saith shall come to pass; he shall have whatsoever he saith.

Mark 11:23

It is time to speak to your mountain. Command the

mountain of sickness, of debt, of problems to give way in Jesus name.

Elijah stopped rain

Elijah stopped rain for three and a half years using unseen elements.

Then he prayed and it rained.

Anyone who can influence the unseen realm does great things.

See his account:

Elias was a man subject to like passions as we are, and he prayed earnestly that it might not rain: and it rained not on the earth by the space of three years and six months.

And he prayed again, and the heaven gave rain, and the earth brought forth her fruit.

James 5:17-18

Glory to God. There are realms we must enter.

If we can influence the unseen, we will do exploits.

We have all it takes to walk in these levels of power, healing sicknesses, stopping the work of the enemy and doing mighty things.

Among the keys that Elijah used to influence the unseen realm are:

Earnest and fervent prayer

Elijah didn't just pray.

The Bible says he prayed earnestly. He prayed passionately.

He prayed with his heart and his might.

That kind of prayer produces serious results.

He was persistent

Elijah prayed 7 times before the rains came down.

There are many who want to influence the unseen realm but give up easily.

Persistence is a strong key to influence the unseen realm.

See the account of Elijah as he pressed on in prayer for rain:

1Ki 18:41 And Elijah said unto Ahab, Get thee up, eat and drink; for there is a sound of abundance of rain.

1Ki 18:42 So Ahab went up to eat and to drink. And Elijah went up to the top of Carmel; and he cast himself down upon the earth, and put his face between his knees,

1Ki 18:43 And said to his servant, Go up now, look toward the sea. And he went up, and looked, and said, There is nothing. And he said, Go again seven times.

1Ki 18:44 And it came to pass at the seventh time, that he said, Behold, there ariseth a little cloud out of the sea, like a man's hand. And he said, Go up, say unto Ahab, Prepare thy chariot, and get thee down, that the rain stop thee not.

1Ki 18:45 And it came to pass in the mean while, that the heaven was black with clouds and wind, and there was a great rain. And Ahab rode, and went to Jezreel.

1 Kings 18:41-45

Elijah took the victory by persistence.

Physical rain appeared through orchestrations in the unseen realm.

May you influence the unseen realm also for

greater physical manifestations.

My desire is to see you progress and prosper and have freedom from negative people and circumstances. Because of that please permit me to introduce two courses that I believe passionately will help you.

1. To cure prayerlessness, an inconsistent prayer life and the pain of not enjoying all that God has made available to you because of the inability to have the prayer life you desire, I have made a course that will help you. Click here to learn more about my 3 Day Course on How to Overcome prayerlessness that will solve the problem of prayerlessness in your life.

2. To overcome the pain of not having enough money to live where you want, eat what you want to eat, do what you want to do and achieve your dreams, I have created a 7 Day Financial Abundance Course that will deliver financial

abundance to you quickly. You too will have the resources to live your dream

Click here to learn more about that course.

Let us conclude in the next chapter

Conclusion

You now know the unseen realm exists.

You have found out about some unseen elements.

It is time to influence the unseen realm in powerful way altogether.

As the title implied, this book is just an introduction to help those who do not know much about the impact of the unseen realm.

The next book in the series has over 100 5-star ratings. It contains the keys to influence the unseen realm for your benefit in the realm of the physical.

You will be empowered to soar to different levels of victory as you read it.

Click the link to get it.

Influencing the unseen realm.

REVIEW

Because your review is important to help others benefit from these books, please leave a good review here

Get these books now and see yourself do exploits. Unseen Realm Series:

1. Influencing the unseen realm

2. Seeing the unseen realm

Manufactured by Amazon.ca
Bolton, ON